MOMMY'S RUNNING FOR OFFICE

MOMMY'S RUNNING FOR OFFICE

Inge W. Horowitz

PathBinder Publishing

Richmond, VA

© Inge W. Horowitz, 2018
Mommy is Running for Office
Published by PathBinder Publishing
ISBN: 978-0-9996048-1-6

Children's Book – All rights reserved. No part of this publication may be reproduced, stored in a retrieval system, or transmitted, in any form or by any means, electronic, mechanical, photocopying, recording or otherwise, without the prior permission of the author.

This is a work of fiction. Names, characters, places and incidents are products of the author's imagination or are used fictitiously. Any similarity to actual persons, organizations, and/or events is purely coincidental.

Published by PathBinder Publishing
www.PathBinderPublishing.com

DEDICATION

This book is dedicated to all the selfless and courageous mothers who run for office.

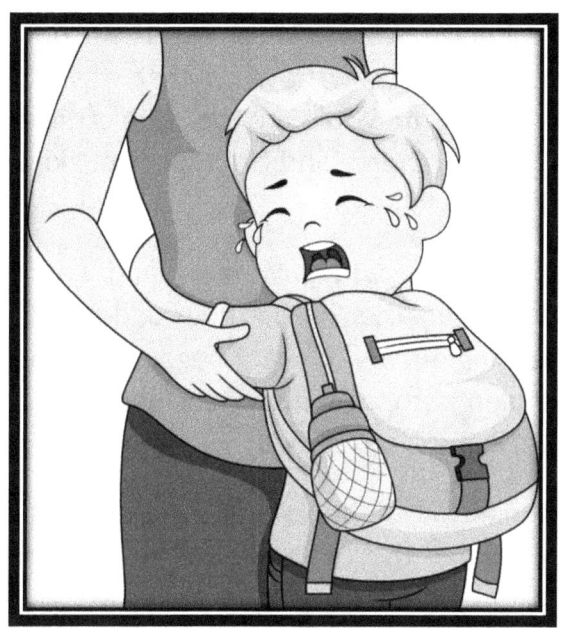

CHAPTER 1

My Mommy is just about my best friend. One day during dinner, Mommy told my Dad, my older brother, Ronin, and me that she wants to run for office.

I asked her how far that is...and she explained that running for office means that she will try to have people elect her or choose her to work at the state capitol in what is called the legislature.

I didn't understand all of that, but I wanted to know how far that was. And when Mommy told me the state capitol is where Grandma and Grandpa live, I knew that was far away.

That night, when Mommy and I were sitting together on the floor and she was reading a story to me, I began to cry and couldn't stop. I didn't want her to go to the capitol, so far away.

And no matter how she explained it to me, all I could think of was that my Mommy, just about my very best friend, would be going far away—if the people chose her. And to think, I don't even know these people.

She explained that it is a great honor to be elected. She said it was good to be a delegate and work in the legislature.

"Mommy, what does elected mean?" I finally had to ask. She used the word so many times, and I was confused.

"Do you remember when I took you with me to vote at your school? Remember that?"

"No, I don't!" The tears made it hard to even see Mommy.

"Sure, you do, honey. Remember how you and I went to the school to vote? And we stood in a little booth behind a curtain, just the two of us. Do you remember that?"

"Oh, yes. Yes, Mommy. Now I remember the curtain." What I remembered was hugging Mommy's legs because it was a little scary behind that dark curtain.

"Well, River, behind that curtain there was a screen with names of three people on it. I was only allowed to vote for one. I chose the person I thought would write laws that would be good for our family and our neighbors, too. That is what's called an **election**. When we went behind that curtain, I voted for my favorite person to represent us. His name was Roger Jones. Well, Mr. Jones got the most votes, and now he is writing laws for us. That's what I want to do, too. So I can help write good laws. You know what a law is, right?"

"Yes, Mommy. It's like when Ronin and I have to be in bed by eight and we have to brush our teeth first."

"Oh, River, you've got it. That's just like it." Mommy gave me a big hug.

"How did you know about Mr. Jones?" I asked.

"I had heard him talk at the school one night and also on television, and I read his letters. I thought that he was smart and honest, and so I voted for him to work for us in the legislature."

"What's the **legislature**?"

"Let me tell you about the legislature. It's a large group of people, called delegates, one from every city and county. Each one had to be elected by their neighbors who live in that city, or county."

Suddenly Mommy jumped up. "I have an idea, River! Tomorrow I am going to take you and Ronin to see the state capitol, the place where I want to work, and we'll watch the delegates, the people who work in the legislature now."

I stopped crying. Mommy kissed me goodnight, and went to tell Ronin about our plan. I snuggled under the covers and fell asleep thinking about going to the state capitol tomorrow.

CHAPTER 2

Ronin and I woke up early the next morning and quickly ate breakfast. We were ready to go with Mommy on our important trip. As we were driving, Mommy began to explain something else.

"First, before the people vote, I must tell them about myself and what I would do for them. You see, boys, the election will happen in November, and right now it's only June."

I slowly counted on my fingers to make sure I did it right. "July, August, September, October, and November. Mommy, that's five months!"

"That's right, River. I'll have five months to tell people about all the ways I want to help. I'll tell them about how I want to make the schools better, and get more doctors to come to our county. We have roads that need repairs and the river is polluted. That is why I am running for office. Five months sounds like a long time, but it will pass by very quickly, you'll see."

I sat back in my seat and soon we came to the city. All of a sudden, there on a hill was the big, white state capitol.

Mommy parked the car in a large garage. She held our hands as we walked over to the capitol. We passed a security guard and stepped into an elevator. Mommy let Ronin push a button that took us up to the third floor.

"Now, boys, we will go into the balcony for visitors where we mustn't talk except maybe whisper very softly like your library voice at school."

We nodded okay.

Mommy, Ronin, and I watched and listened to the people below. I didn't understand what they were talking about. After a little while we stood up and left quietly.

Driving home, we stopped at a park with tables and ate our lunch. While eating our sandwiches, Mommy suddenly exclaimed, "Boys, I have a great idea! All summer, while you are out of school, you two can help me get elected!"

"Like what could we do?" Ronin asked.

"School will be over in two weeks, but I'll let you start right away. Next Monday evening we'll eat dinner early. Then we will go to my friend Mary's house and work on my campaign. I'll take you boys with me, and you'll see, there will be something for both of you to do. Maybe you could count envelopes or learn to fold letters. Or you could serve cookies and napkins to the people talking on their cell phones."

"That'll be fun!" Ronin and I shouted together.

I was starting to get excited about Mommy running for office.

CHAPTER 3

Monday morning when Mommy dropped us off at school, I told Ms. Turner, my teacher, that I would be helping Mommy get elected. Guess what she said? "That's great, River! Last week my friend made phone calls for your Mommy. Everyone should learn about the people who are running for office and get involved, even young people. I am proud of you, River!"

I couldn't wait for the last school bell to ring. We ate dinner at five o'clock, and then Mommy drove Ronin and me straight to Mary's house. There were a lot of people there helping to do things. One man was working on a computer. A lady was counting out envelopes. Behind the door of every bedroom, there was someone on a cell phone. I heard them talking about Mommy and how she can help write new laws that would make things better for all of us.

A nice lady named Rena came over and told me she needed me to help her in the den. She showed me how to fold a letter into three parts. I practiced on a few until I figured out just where to make the folds. She said I was doing a great job, and I could be her helper. So, I folded letters and she stuffed them into envelopes. Rena said the letters told about all the things that Mommy wanted to do when she got to be a delegate.

Wow! I felt so proud that I could help all summer! Mommy took both of us every Monday night when she went to Mary's house. Mommy signed letters while Ronin and I kept busy helping.

CHAPTER 4

The next Saturday Mommy took Ronin and me to knock on doors. When someone opened the door, she introduced the three of us. She told them she was running for office to help make the schools and roads better in our district. Then she asked if we could put up a yard sign, with her name on it, on their front lawn. When they said, "Okay," Ronin and I ran to the car and got a yard sign and stuck it into the ground. Two nice people even came out to help. They carried a bunch of signs so that we wouldn't have to run back to the car every time.

After that, we went with Mommy almost every Monday night and Saturday to help. And now guess what? I'm so glad that Mommy's running for office!

Finally, election day came and we were in front of my school. People were coming to vote. Mommy was shaking hands and thanking them for coming. Ronin and I handed out sample ballots. Each one had Mommy's name in letters that were bigger and darker than the other names.

That night, my whole family watched the election results on TV. At last, at 11 o'clock the news man announced that Mommy had won!

I hugged her tighter than I think I have ever hugged her before.

A few weeks later Ronin and I missed school so that we could watch Mommy get sworn in. I was never soooooooooooo happy and proud! That night for dinner, Ronin and I got extra ice cream to celebrate!

About the Author

Inge Windmueller Horowitz has enjoyed careers in occupational therapy and as an educational consultant for the Virginia Department of Education, assessing children with learning problems in the Department of Child Neurology at the Medical College of Virginia.

Since her retirement, Inge has tutored children, volunteered as a mentor for ten years at an inner city elementary school, coordinated the *Learning Disabilities Directory*, co-edited the book, *Understanding Learning Disabilities*, and volunteered as executive director of the Learning Disabilities Council.

Inge was president of the Emek Sholom Holocaust Memorial Cemetery from 1995 until 2015. She has been active at the Virginia Holocaust Museum since its founding, developing the Survivor Room, conducting videotaped interviews of survivors and WWII veterans, and serving as a docent. As her family's historian, Inge, her mother and daughter produced the *Windmueller Family Chronicle*, and helped to organize two worldwide family reunions.

Inge was married to Harold Horowitz for 66 years when he passed away in January, 2017. They have two children, five grandchildren, and two great-grandchildren.

For more children's book ideas, and other fiction and nonfiction genres, visit PathBinder Publishing at: www.PathBinderPublishing.com

www.ingramcontent.com/pod-product-compliance
Lightning Source LLC
LaVergne TN
LVHW021750060526
838200LV00052B/3568